THOU SHALL NOT DIE

Other titles of interest from St. Augustine's Press

THOU SHALL NOT DIE

By Gabriel Marcel

Selected and Arranged by Anne Marcel
Translated by Katharine Rose Hanley
Introduced by Xavier Tilliette, S.J.

ST. AUGUSTINE'S PRESS
South Bend, Indiana
2009

Manufactured in the United States of America.

1 2 3 4 5 6 14 13 12 11 10 09

Library of Congress Cataloging in Publication Data
Marcel, Gabriel, 1889–1973.
[Tu ne mourras pas. English]
Thou shall not die / by Gabriel Marcel; selected and
arranged by Anne Marcel; translated by Katharine Rose
Hanley; introduced by Xavier Tilliette, S.J.
p. cm.
Includes bibliographical references (p.   ) and index.
ISBN-13: 978-1-58731-861-0 (hardcover: alk. paper)
ISBN-10: 1-58731-861-X (hardcover: alk. paper)
1. Marcel, Gabriel, 1889–1973 – Quotations.
I. Marcel, Anne. II. Title.
B2430.M252E5 2008
194 – dc22   2008035177

∞ *The paper used in this publication meets the minimum require-*
ments of the American National Standard for Information Sciences –
Permanence of Paper for Printed Materials, ANSI Z39.48-1984.

St. Augustine's Press
www.staugustine.net

Contents

Notes to the Present Text

The excerpts presented in this work are drawn in part from unpublished manuscripts and in part from various published works of Gabriel Marcel: *Etre et Avoir (Being and Having); Essai de philosophie concrète (Creative Fidelity); Homo Viator (Homo Viator); Pour une sagesse tragique (Tragic Wisdom and Beyond); Présence et Immortalité (Presence and Immortality); Le Monde cassé (The Broken World);* and *Le Dard (The Sting).*

L'Association Gabriel Marcel – 21, rue de Tournon, 75006 Paris, tel. 01 43 26 84 32 – has fortunately reedited a certain number of works by the philosopher which had become unavailable (notably *Être et avoir, le Mystère de l'Être, Homo Viator, l'Homme problématique,* as well as *Entretiens entre Paul Ricoeur et Gabriel Marcel,* and a collective work published under the direction of Etienne Fouilloux, *Un intellectuel en son siècle*).

Preface

This volume scarcely needs an introduction, nor is setting its historic context necessary. The book speaks for itself and, if simply read, offers a richness of profound reflections that touch the soul.

Still, the presence of a philosopher in a collection of texts concerning spirituality might surprise the reader. Thus, at the start of the presentation, some clarification is appropriate.

We must recall that this philosopher is primarily the same little boy who asked the adults in his life: "Where are those who have died?" The grownups replied that they did not know. "Well then," said the child, "when I grow up, I shall seek to find out . . ."

The grown man did not betray the child's promise. As a student, then as a young professor of philosophy, Gabriel Marcel consecrated his reflections principally on themes most intimately affecting our life: What is the relation between memory and presence, and between knowledge and faith?

For the next twenty years spiritual experience was central to his preoccupations without his ever considering himself to be a Christian.

It was at the age of thirty-nine that he first came to the awareness of being on the way to Christ and, seeking to grow that belief, he joined the Roman Catholic Church. There he found his true faith community to which, in spite of everything, he remained faithful unto his dying breath.

His reflection taught him to understand one thing: our faith can only be real to the extent it is received as grace, and not conquered through meditation. The light of God convinced him that it is the Spirit Himself who, joined to our own spirits, attests that we are all children of God and enables us to finally cry out: *Abba, Father!*

From the years following World War II in Europe until the end of his life, his meditations led him to search out what it is that constitutes the foundation of human dignity: "It is characteristic of people of good will" he wrote, "that whatever their religion may be, they continually open themselves more and more to one another, and in this way work to establish, or to strengthen, this Mystical Body which remains, for me, the supreme exigency of a free and believing conscience."

Faced with the increasing dehumanization at work in his contemporary world, this philosopher found his response in the spiritual resources of a man of faith, a response needed in our current times more than ever.

Anne Marcel

Threshold Introduction

Though he was in no way marginal to the world of philosophy, Gabriel Marcel did not follow the more frequent pattern of a philosopher's lifestyle, namely that of teaching at universities. Instead his was the lifestyle of solitary thinker like Solomon Maimon, Baader, Kierkegaard, or Schopenhauer. Thus free from routine requirements in an educational environment, he could dedicate himself to study and reflection. Yet, despite his independent style, he and his work attained considerable influence and notoriety, equal to that of any of the great masters.

This independence did not hamper Marcel's investigations; rather it corresponded well with his temperament of spontaneity, vitality, and directness of experience. Avoiding pedantry, or mere show or erudition, his thought was intuitive and penetrating. He enjoyed direct short paths, but also long ambling walks. He also had several spheres of creative interest. Among these theatre was his preference, but he also had a gift for music, literature, drama criticism, and translation, although philosophy remained his principal occupation.

His heuristic thought found diverse forms of expression, but preferably in the form of a journal, which is well suited to ruminations and an attention ever alert. His journals, exempt of confidences, are a dialogue with himself, yet having constantly in view other interlocutors. It was in writing his *Metaphysical Journal* that the young agrégé, although familiar with academic fashions, became aware of an incorrigible allergy to "systems" and systematic expositions.

Effectively his brief reflections often run vagabond and take unforeseeable detours; however, they never come up empty, as most of his sketches are the first drafts for articles or lectures. Already the first *Metaphysical Journal* assembled the material of a thesis.

Gabriel Marcel's style of investigation, always explorative and alert, is that of a person *en route*, which he has made the category *par excellence* of his thought. That is why the beautiful invocation of *The Spirit of Metamorphosis*, which frames this collection, is a sort of talisman for the entire work.

The *Journal*, as we have said, calls out to another interlocutor and the dyad is another major category of our author.

Gabriel Marcel is a philosopher of dialogue. Having taught only briefly, he made up for the absence of regular student audiences with meetings, conversations, the famous Friday evening gatherings, and his frequent welcoming of writers.

He drew eagerly from his theatrical work to provide examples, also circumstances and current events constantly brought their own weight to his questioning.

Few people, especially of an advanced age, would have been as attentive, as vibrantly in touch with those present and to trends in world events as he was. This is what infuses his work with freshness, a personal vitality, which makes it apt, as Etienne Gilson observed, always to create new friends.

* * * * *

The direction of his work – fundamentally ethical, even familial – is simple, even though expressed through various works. It starts with the fundamental situation which is human embodiment, incarnate existence, oscillating between having and being, and during all its development, in which chronology has little importance, it is attracted or polarized by "the mystery of being," being as mystery. Despite the increasing importance of being, which becomes more important than existence, it is "mystery" which is really important and which imprints its mark on the itinerary.

Mystery is distinguishable in contrast to problems, and thus it is not accessible with the normal and habitual means of intelligence, that is to say the categories of logic and metaphysics, rehabilitated by Maritain and by Gilson. Thus Marcel's invention of new notions like reflection, invocation, presence, witness, piety . . . recovered by the *"second reflection,"* the true instrument of a concrete philosophy, issued from a "reprise" or by an existential leap.

But this "*methodology of the unverifiable*" (Pietro Prini) would remain sterile without the constant contribution of the dyadic. It is the *Thou*, it is that love of the other, that opens the door of hope, and which gives access to a symphonic universe, to the *"communion in the light"* for which we all have a nostalgic longing.

However, the lighthearted and tireless thinking is not without its somber and sometimes tragic dark side, which his theatre brings to light. His thought is a victory, a conquest over despair and possible betrayal- his thought escapes the "trinity of evil" of technical absolutism, the collectivity, and the abstract.

His thought is founded on the great category of the trial, which is like a "judgment of God." But this is not confronted without the viaticum of hope and the ultimate recourse, the vision of sanctity, of which the glimpsed face of Christ offers the shining paradigm.

Such are, summarily indicated, the rubrics according to which, in the following pages, one will find the authentic accent of a thinker whose lifelike and personal style of writing give his testimony an incomparable power.

Xavier Tilliette, S.J.

Meditation

Spirit of metamorphosis,

when we try to push back the veil of clouds
which separates us from the other realm,
guide our novice gesture!

And when the appointed hour chimes, awaken in us
the light-hearted spirit of the traveler, who fastens
*   on his sack,*
while outside the misted windows there appears
the gentle dawning of daybreak!

I consider myself as having been a philosopher of the threshold, a philosopher who, I must admit, placed himself, rather uncomfortably, on the frontier between believers and unbelievers, in order, in that way, to be able to draw on the backing of believers, on Christian religion, and on the Catholic religion, but in such a manner as to be able to speak with non-believers, so I can make myself understood by them and perhaps even assist them.

* * * * *

I would be inclined to deny a properly philosophic quality to any work in which one cannot discern what I shall call "the bite of reality."

I would also add that in the development of a philosophy, there occurs, unfortunately, a point after which the tool of dialectic argument tends to operate exclusively in a void.

* * * * *

Affecting thought, there is a kind of staleness, resembling stagnant water: only, this stagnation hides itself under a flow of words or, what amounts to the same thing, ready-made ideas, which no longer are thoughts.

This happens constantly among professional rhetoricians and, also too frequently, one must admit, among preachers.

Phrases automatically follow one another, dictated by a mechanism, which, in fact, is habit.

On the contrary, the current of thought flows only where the mind develops a certain power of invention or of creativity.

* * * * *

Leftover scraps from philosophic thought clutter all minds, more or less; stale slogans spread by newspapers, by digests, or simply by conversations. Most of the time these scraps could be advantageously burnt like household garbage, and it is not one of philosophy's least important tasks to proceed with this sort of incineration.

Once and for all, we have to dispose of the model of a window or a display case, where different philosophers would be placed one beside another so that a client has only to make a choice among them. Such a comparison is absurd, because juxtaposition like that is possible only for objects or things. A philosophy can by no means be treated in such a way, for philosophy is, in a certain manner, an experience. I would even say an adventure, within a much larger adventure, that of thought as a whole, or even at the heart of something that transcends even that whole adventure, if it's the manifestation of the Spirit and the Word, if it's a theophany.

* * * * *

In every thinking being there occurs, not continuously but from time to time, a sort of rudiment of philosophic experience. I would willingly say that such an experience presents itself as a sort of trembling awe in the presence of those great mysterious realities which confer on every human life its concrete setting: love, death, the birth of a child . . . As for me, I do not hesitate to say, that every emotion personally felt in contact with these realities is the embryo of philosophic experience. Almost every human being has experienced, at certain privileged moments, this need – to be enlightened, to receive a response to his own questioning.

* * * * *

Nothingness. Can nothingness be considered as the background from which being comes to be present?

I ask myself if nothingness doesn't have an intermediary and suspect role between an initial position and an ulterior position of being. I admit that I find it repugnant to admit any sort of primacy to nothingness. I believe that this is false psychologically. Metaphysically I do not believe that it can be maintained for a single moment.

In other words, I do not think that one can seriously say: the problem of being implies a certain priority of the problem of nothingness. I believe that nothingness is rather something sub-sequent or ulterior.

* * * * *

Admiration. The verb *to lift up* emphasizes strong-ly and in a most exact and meaningful manner the type of action that admiration exerts upon us.

This is so true that when hearing a poetic or musical work, for example, we express our enthusi-asm to someone who does not share it, not only does it seem to us that the other is earthbound while we are flying, but we can have the very painful impression that he drags us down, that he makes us stumble, and the violence with which we protest against the other's attitude is in some way a measure of the effort with which we resist him.

It is certain that, first of all, it is proper to admiration to draw us out of ourselves, away from the thought or preoccupation with ourselves; admiration is the active negation of a certain inner inertia.

Admiration can be conceived not only as a certain surge but also as an eruption (the verb *to inundate* here corresponds to an undeniable reali-ty). This eruption can only arise at the center or heart of a being who does not form, with himself or herself, a hermetically closed system, into which something new can no longer penetrate.

The ideas of admiration and of revelation are, in reality, correlative.

* * * * *

Courage is the virtue without which a person denies the truth of who she or he is. Courage consists, above all, in looking into the truth of reality. It is opposed to deception in all its forms, not only to deception, but also to feigning. Yet we know that the slave is condemned to pretend and feign. We who have suffered from an enemy occupation, have only to recall the fraud of every kind that we were condemned to by the presence of the enemy on our soil – to the point that one could come to consider them not only as excusable, but as required obligations.

In this sense, it is incontestable that any occupation by the enemy is a school for immorality.

From the Secret to the Mysterious

Each of us is sufficiently in touch with our childhood to relive the exaltation experienced in those early years, not only to find that he holds a secret, but even more to show before another – a friend, a brother, sometimes even before one's parents – the superiority this possession confers on him. For surely it's a possession we're speaking about, as ennobling as that may be. How could a secret not be treated as something one possesses and of which others are deprived?

* * * * *

But one would omit something essential in ignoring the contrast, agreeably experienced by the one who holds the secret, between his or her own richness and the deprivation of the uninitiated. What is most striking here is the analogy between the secret and its hiding place; there is no need here to invoke the symbolism abused by fanatics of psychoanalysis. What matters in both cases is the presence of a magical element; it is the accessing of something invisible, or even to employ a metaphysical term overused to the point that no one any longer discerns its exact meaning, transcendence in its most primitive form.

The child, concealed in his hiding place, experiences a veritable giddiness to observe those who search for him. The child sees without being seen. The child is right there, not one of their movements escapes his gaze; we believe we hear that kind of ecstatic and poorly repressed giggling of a small child who cannot succeed in mastering his glee. This is because he participates in the privilege which inhabitants of the invisible world enjoy, to whom it is given to spy on us, but whose presence, alas, is revealed to us only by fleeting and uncertain signs.

In the strongest sense of the word, isn't one justified in saying that the invisible being is transcendent? What is marvelous is that he is, at one and the same time, here and elsewhere. He is among those who try in vain to catch hold of him, but at the same time he is beyond, since he is endowed with a privilege, and for others this privilege can only be the object of suspicion.

The possessor of a secret enjoys a similar situation. As for me, I know something that you don't, and about which others too are ignorant. I will be careful not to reveal my secret to you, besides it's not my right to, and I have every reason to be proud of the confidence shown me by the one who has confided this secret to me. But even if I were authorized to divulge this secret, I would abstain from doing so. I'm experiencing too lively a pleasure in seeing you prowl around, hazarding hypotheses, each one appearing to me who know the truth, as more foolish and more amusing than the others.

A remarkable phenomenon is the kind of affective glow that shines at the surface of my secret (again likened to a charm that I would carry on me) from the first of the suppositions that come to brush up against its resistant surface. These guesses appear as awkward approaches, sometime as casts of fishing nets.

Thus the secret situates itself for the child, at the center, as a sort of ballet which brings joy to his heart. But almost always there is a moment when the child conceals his secret, draping himself protectively over it, covering it, wrapping it in a ferociously defensive silence.

There is dialectic of the secret that reason has no trouble discovering. My secret has value in my eyes only if you are aware of its existence while still remaining ignorant as to what its nature is. It becomes more real to the extent that you struggle to penetrate it. But is it not impossible that eventually you actually do penetrate it? So, I cannot but wish that you give up trying to unveil this secret; however if you lose interest, if it ceases to fascinate you, it will be as if it no longer existed; that would be for the secret a manner of burning itself out like a fuse.

Wouldn't that finally be the tragedy that hovers over all possessions no matter what they may be?

Considered in their being as possessions, don't they borrow the best of what they are in the light of a covetousness that shines from the depth of another's eyes?

* * * * *

These remarks are nonetheless far from revealing the entire nature of a secret's essence. Only a child, or an adult who still bears certain stigma of infantilism, delights in arousing in another a curiosity that the child has decided, in advance, not to satisfy.

One may say that in a mature person, a secret is less and less comparable to an object one holds under lock and key, because it is more and more intimately lived. Thus, for example, if I am the holder of information confided to me under the seal of secrecy, I will know very well that if I want to keep my promise, I must then guard myself from showing that I have been made privy to something that has been forbidden me to reveal.

To boast about a confidence entrusted to me would already be in a certain way to have betrayed it. That is to say, so no one can identify my secret I should not let it shine even from a distance. I am expected to incorporate it. It must be, that buried within me; it becomes an aspect of me.

Perhaps it may even become necessary for me to give up the habit of formulating it to myself. For so long as I keep repeating it, I keep open the possibility, consequently the temptation to divulge it and pass it on. As resolute as I may be to not reveal the secret, there remains in it a germ of death for so long as I have not succeeded in absorbing it into my own substance. Hence an antagonism at once real and refrained between the tendency of secrets to reveal and spread themselves, and ones will to remain master of that temptation.

* * * * *

Yet actually the real secret is not the one someone else has confided to me: doesn't each one of us have at the center of our self a domain which belongs to one's self alone, and which one protects with jealous care against any possible intrusions? Although at certain times one may experience an itching to divulge it; but to divulge it, wouldn't that be a manner of extinguishing the flame which consumes him?

Now it appears clearly that an authentic secret is not something one has, that it is in no way comparable to a jewel that one takes out of a box to show one day to onlookers. Perhaps, as the cynical psychologist would say, in the hope of awakening the envy deep within the heart of another, we will again find that ferocious trembling that shuddered within us when we first decided to acquire that gem or that piece of costume jewelry.

The more the secret is truly ours, the more it is authentic – the more we understand that the divulging of it is not only undesirable, but actually impossible. Divulged, it would change its nature. This is all the more true as our deepest, most intimate secret is without doubt the one we don't even succeed in communicating to ourselves.

That very secret is the one that separates me from myself, at least from the frivolous and buzzing stooges which at certain times transform my soul into an aviary until the moment when the master of that place imposes silence on them. I then find the painful solitude which takes hold of us after certain receptions, as if the room, profaned by so many commonplace comments or useless paradoxes, had silently aspired toward some unfeasible purification.

It is just there, at its final limit, that the secret joins and merges with mystery. This mystery of myself which only a science without brains or a philosophy without heart would persist in denying; it's a secret if you will – but its key has not been given to me, and perhaps doesn't exist anywhere. For it would be infantile, it would even be sacrilegious to think that the One who is more interior to me than I am to myself is similar to a homeowner who, through caution, has abstained from giving, to seasonal or yearly renters, the key to the cupboard where the family jewels are hidden.

If in truth we do belong to a mystery, then it's precisely that imagery, so easy to invoke for the sake of edification, which is falsifying and completely untrue. The highest wisdoms, the greatest mystics of whatever traditions, seem to have all recognized: God dwells in us as a host, and that for the duration of all time, short of an eschatological rupture that it's vain to want to imagine. He intended that this dwelling place, which has been given to me, remain mine until the sacred instant when it will explode into pieces.

* * * * *

But if it is so intimately *my home*, how is it that at certain times it seems to me to be irreducibly mysterious?

That's because it is haunted, perhaps angelically haunted; but the mystery consists in the fact that no knowledge of any order can explain the relations that bond us to a Host whose presence in us lets itself be glimpsed only in brief flashes.

Only poetry, in a most exceptional way, and above all music, can try to evoke, the one by way of allusion, the other by its own incantations, the veiled star, whose gentle rays all together familiar and intermittent, never obscures itself lastingly for a soul, unless that soul surrenders itself to idols that hold sway over the deserts of the heart.

Mystery

Knowledge exiles to infinity all it claims to embrace . . . Perhaps it is mystery alone that reunites.

Without mystery, life would be unlivable.

* * * * *

One might believe that grace is impenetrable to all reflection; but this is true only of an elementary first reflection, one incapable of reflecting on itself.

Yet where reflection exercises itself in its fullness, it comes to recognize that it derives from something which surpasses it and makes it possible.

This assurance is mysterious, but that by no means implies that it is obscure. Quite the opposite, it means that reflection proceeds from light, and in a certain sense, is light.

* * * * *

"A person seeks for truth by reason alone, and that person fails; truth is offered to that person by faith [and], he accepts it; and having accepted it, he finds it satisfies reason."

Paradox? If one wishes to say so. For my part, I am inclined to think that there is no Christian philosophy except where this paradox, this scandal, is not merely admitted, accepted, but *embraced* with boundless gratitude and without reserve.

* * * * *

Distinction between the mysterious and the problematic. A problem is something that one bumps into, which blocks the way. It is completely before me. On the contrary, a mystery is something in which I find myself engaged, whose essence is therefore not to be entirely before me.

It's as if in this zone, the distinction between *"in me"* and *"before me,"* loses all significance.

* * * * *

One night, in Lyon, many years ago, at a very painful moment in my life, a thought suddenly dawned on me:

"To abstain from praying is to refuse to let oneself be loved."

That thought came to me by surprise, to me for whom prayer had always been particularly difficult. It all happened as if it came from somewhere else, from on high, as if I needed to scrutinize its meaning.

It is obvious that this thought would be meaningless if, as people all too frequently believe, prayer were above all a request. But how can we deny that prayer can also be, and more essentially be, thanksgiving, that is to say a transport toward; and can't one understand that it is through this uplifting, because of this uplifting, and thanks to this uplifting, that God can become present to us. And if we remain closed off unto ourselves, if we give into a feeling of irremediable solitude, it's as if we do not allow God to give Himself to us in the very act whereby we raise ourselves toward Him.

I acknowledge moreover very simply that these thoughts are difficult, that they require an effort, and that perhaps there is a sort of merit in entertaining them, that is to say, finally, to struggle against that inertia which, alas, is ours, and which is the expression, perhaps vague or indistinct, but significant, of sin.

* * * * *

In this world that we see being built up around us, at a speed surpassing that of vital growth, or organic developments, we find beings are all the more isolated as they are more closely crowded together.

Proximity is in no way the source of fraternity. And it is not by chance that too much proximity is accompanied by a deafening din, such that no one, any longer, feels at home.

Solitude is essential for fraternity as silence is essential to music. Let us note that fraternity is first, above all, a form of respect, and that there is no respect without distance, which means that every human being needs an interior space without which that individual will inevitably wither like a plant, or like a tree.

* * * * *

Wisdom . . . clarification of the notion of wisdom . . . through a paradox that is only apparent, one must recognize that the practical problem and the metaphysical problem tend to intermingle. I mean to say that it would not be enough to exhume such and such a principle from the past, which would only represent a reconstructive value on the condition of becoming incarnate; and this incarnation can occur only to the most humble and intimate of human existence, where several persons of good will meet with one another to accomplish a common task.

I realize that this call to humility sounds somewhat disappointing in an age such as ours, when the term "worldwide" is in some way invoked whenever one tries to establish any kind of organization whatsoever. But it's just that habit and pretentiousness which is the mark of one of the most pernicious illusions there could be, hope to enter gradually, through our individual trials, unforeseeable for each one of us yet still inseparable from each one's own vocation.

I hope in Thee for us.

A Light That Would Be Joy to Be Light

To give something is not simply to pass it from one

place to another; it is to transform it by incorporating into it something of oneself.

The gift that was given to me, if it is truly a gift, doesn't add itself to a preexistent collection of possessions. It is situated on another level, that of testimony. It is a pledge of friendship or of love.

It is this only on condition of being recognized as such. In this respect it can be likened to an appeal, to which there should be a mode of welcome as response.

* * * * *

The soul of the gift is generosity: a light that would be joy to be light.

The essence of light is to be illuminating, illuminating for others. . . . If it is joy in being light, it can only will to be light increasingly.

Like a flame, generosity nourishes itself.

* * * * *

Recollection, as a renewal of contact with the source, emits a light (which can in no way be confused with the clarity of what we can call understanding).

Recollection gives us certain resources for the interior journey we have to make in the direction of that event beyond representation toward which we move, in an almost complete obscurity.

How is the recognition of a mystery possible, if not by the favor of an interior retrieval? It is linked to the act by which the subject creates silence within himself or herself. It is in recollection, and only in recollection, that it is appropriate to seek a refuge.

One could say that mystery and recollection are correlatives. There is no ontology possible, that is to say no apprehension of the mystery of being, to any degree whatsoever, except for a being capable of recollection and of witnessing, by that very act, that he or she is not a pure and simple living being, a creature at the mercy of his life, given over to it without any grip on it.

Now at the same time one must recognize that every action, inasmuch as it is a choice, is a mutilation, and one could even say, an injury done to reality. The human tragedy consists, on the one hand, that each one of us is condemned to perform that mutilation, for it is only on that condition that one becomes oneself. But also, inasmuch, as one is bound to make up for that fault, if it is one, by a sort of compensatory action, which consists basically in the restoration of the unity that he contributed to breaking by his choice.

One might ask oneself if this compensatory value doesn't confer its deepest sense to the religious act as this is expressed in prayer or recollection, but also by the poet or by the artist.

* * * * *

Light – that is to say at the convergence of truth and love. This light we must radiate toward one another, knowing very well that our role consists above all, and perhaps even exclusively, in not being an obstacle to its passage *through us*.

Despite appearances, it's an active role because my self is a pretension, and this pretension is called to overcome or break itself, which is only possible through one's liberty, that which *is* liberty.

* * * * *

The best of me does not belong to me; I am in no way its owner, only its depository.

What is important is to know what attitude I shall adopt toward my gifts. If I consider them as a deposit that I am bound to render fruitful, that is to say, at best, as the expression of a call given to me, or even sometimes a question that was addressed to me – I will not dream of being puffed up with pride and showing off in front of others, that is to say in front of myself.

When I really reflect upon it, there is nothing in me that cannot and should not be regarded as a gift.

* * * * *

Sacrifice is, in itself, foolishness; but a deeper reflection permits recognizing the value of such foolishness and understanding that if a person were to refuse it, he would sink beneath himself.

My life, when I sacrifice it, is not some thing that I abandon to obtain some other thing. It's a whole.

However, there must be something beyond this whole, something which must be safeguarded at all costs; otherwise the sacrifice would be without any meaning.

At the root of the absolute sacrifice, one finds not only, *"I die,"* but, *"Thou, thou shall not die."*

* * * * *

What a rudimentary and false psychology is the one that represents the sacrifice of the believer as the consequence of a careful calculation! Rather, it is carried by a current of hope and love.

It is by starting with the *"consecrated soul"* that one comes to dissipate these secular misunderstandings. One sees then that the consecrated soul is at the same time inhabited by an invincible hope; it aspires to enter with its God into an intimacy ever greater, ever more complete . . .

On Being as the Place of Fidelity

At the very depth of ourselves, we don't know what is happening. We don't even know if anything is happening. We throw the net of our interpretations into depths that are impenetrable in every respect. . . . We draw out only phantasms, or at least, we cannot be sure that they may be anything else.

Still, there are not only inexplorable waters. There is the world of light. There we no longer draw out; it is we who are drawn in! This world, it is the world of grace; it becomes more and more direct, increasingly consistent to the extent that we believe in it more and more completely, and this belief cannot be illusory, for the images that it uses it breaks immediately thereafter to find others.

* * * * *

Fidelity is the opposite of inert conformity. It is the active recognition of a certain presence, or of something in us and before us as a presence, but which, *ipso facto*, can also very well be misunderstood, forgotten, or obliterated. We see appear here the shadow of betrayal, which, in my opinion, envelopes our entire human world like a sinister cloud.

* * * * *

Despair and betrayal are there lying in wait for us and seeking to trap us at every moment; and death at the end of our visible career, as a permanent invitation to absolute defection, as an incitement to proclaim that nothing exists, that nothing has worth.

* * * * *

(Lament of a woman rendered desperate by the death of her son.) *"He does nothing but repeat phrases about the will of God, and its impenetrable ways. He only gives me straw when what I need is bread!*

"He had the audacity to say to me: With time . . . Time! He said: To heal . . . *As if I didn't weep for my poor dear Maurice just as bitterly as the first day. Those men haven't lived. They have seen others suffer however; they have received other people's confidences, but one would say that these were lost in the sands of their certitude, a desiccated certitude."*

* * * * *

Everything obliges us to recognize that fidelity,

even toward oneself, is difficult to discern and practice; to be faithful to oneself one must remain alive, and that is not an easy thing . . .

Contrary to what one might have thought, my presence to myself doesn't happen automatically; instead it is subject to eclipses, and must always be reconquered.

If someone were to ask what this presence is, what is this self to which it is so difficult to remain faithful? the reply must be that it is the parcel of creation that is in me, the gift which was given to me from all eternity, to participate in the universal drama, to work for example to humanize the Earth – or on the contrary, to render it more uninhabitable . . .

* * * * *

The fact of purely and simply conserving does not imply spiritual justification; fidelity only presents a value to the extent in which it assures the persistence or lasting quality of a soul or of a love.

But soul and love are living things whose life is in perpetual renewal. That is to say that one completely misunderstands the sense and value of fidelity if one sees it as a form of inertia; fidelity is and must remain a flame.

But this flame could not be able to burn in a vacuum; it is called to become incarnate in acts and in works which give witness to it.

* * * * *

What must be brought to light is the fact that love, in the fullest and most concrete sense of the word, the love of one person for another, seems to have as its basis the unconditional: *"I shall continue to love you no matter what happens."*

One could even say that love, far beyond saying it implies the acceptance of risk, demands it: it's as if love calls for a test over which it is sure to triumph.

* * * * *

Fidelity involves a fundamental ignorance of the future. I don't know, in pledging fidelity to another, what kind of a future awaits us, and even in a sense what kind of a person this other will be tomorrow; and it's this very ignorance that confers upon my oath its value and its weight.

The only victory overcoming time participates in fidelity. (A very profound word of Nietzsche's: *"A human is the only being who can make promises."*)

* * * * *

Fidelity cannot be separated from an oath, that is to say that it implies the consciousness of the sacred. I commit myself to not abandoning you, and this commitment is the more sacred in my eyes as I subscribe to it more freely, and you would have less recourse against me if I were to break it.

I know moreover that, by the very fact that I shall thus bind myself absolutely, the means will be given to me to keep my faith: this oath, which very well in its origin and in its essence may be my act, or more profoundly, *because* it is my act, becomes thereby the strongest barrier there could be against everything in me that tends toward laxity and dissolution.

* * * * *

Faith is not something one has, not something one owns or possesses, it is not a privilege: or else how could we bear the sight of those to whom this gift had been refused?

No, it does not allow itself to be treated this way except from the moment when we begin to betray it, when we say: *"We others . . . we Catholics . . . we Christians . . ."*

Words that should never be said!

* * * * *

Viewed from without, any fidelity appears incomprehensible, impracticable, a gamble, and scandalous. One asks how could this man have been faithful to that fat person with a snub nose, or to that bloodless bean-pole, or that blue-stocking bookworm?

What, seen from without, appears like a vicious circle is experienced from within as growth, as deepening, or as ascension. We are, in the order of what cannot really be given, as a spectacle, neither to others, nor to ourselves.

* * * * *

Memory is not a simple conservation; one must rather regard it as a vigil, a vigilance of the attentive soul. That vigilance is an active struggle against the forces of inner dispersion, let us say of distraction.

Forgetting is a lack of fidelity. One must always remember that fidelity is active, that it is the opposite of inertia.

Dialogue on Fidelity

One of your most enlightening studies, which profoundly affected several young men before 1939, focuses on clarifying creative fidelity. It was as shocking when it appeared as was creative evolution. When one thinks of *evolution*, one doesn't think of *creation*, and inversely, when one thinks of *fidelity*, one thinks of *conservation*, *persistence*, not of *creation*. What is the real place of this sentiment, of this existential movement in your thought?

I think it is absolutely central. These words were imposed on me probably by a reflection on the notion of promises kept. It became absolutely essential, and I could observe that, in certain cases, this creative fidelity was able to help some people to live.

Let's take the example of someone who, leaving for a long journey, comes to entrust his child to a friend . . . For the friend, fidelity doesn't consist in returning to the traveler, when he comes back, the child exactly as that child was at the moment of departure. There were initiatives to take for his education, for his health, and it would have been on the contrary showing himself unfaithful to say: *"Ah! But I don't want to take any initiative, one might say it's like an object that I must return exactly as it was, just like a ring stored in a desk or dresser drawer."*

I think that this notion of creative initiatives as an expression of fidelity is a very important notion, and I'll go even much further; I think that the mystery of the Church cannot understand itself without starting from this idea. –

Can't your parable possibly be reduced to that of the talents in the Gospel? But in that case that productivity in fidelity isn't as shocking? Inversely, isn't there also a unilateral fidelity when it's a question of something infinitely precious, which, perhaps, would be external and which, by this fact, absolutely does not allow for productivist metaphors which you have, in that case, connected to creation?

I don't see why that productivity would be shocking. What seems shocking to me, is to use the word *productivity* at all. I chose the word *initiative*, which is quite less displeasing.

Now, I think there are cases where, effectively, fidelity doesn't imply any sort of transformation, for example, fidelity to one's given word. It is quite true that in a case of this sort, one cannot speak of creation, but for me it's a *"cas limit"* a case at the extreme limit, for I think that fidelity is something that has a sort of efficiency, a sort of efficaciousness. That is the way it has always appeared to me.

The Encounter with Evil

Here I would like to proceed with what I would willingly call an *experience of thinking* in the spirit of existential philosophy: that means that I will not proceed with an analysis focused on a notion, but that I will ask myself how we human beings encounter Evil, and what it is possible to say about this encounter.

* * * * *

Reflecting with some students in the past, I always invited them, after they had presented their expositions, to do something unusual, namely to dramatize the situation.

"*Let us Imagine,*" I said to them, *"a particular human being, finding himself caught up in a problem like the one we have been talking about – let us say a problem of responsibility – and let us ask ourselves if what you said just now could be of any help to him,*

*that is to say, could it help him to orient himself in this
sort of night in which he's been struggling?*

*"But to reply to this question, you would have to
put yourself in the place of this particular individual;
to cease being simply a lecturer speaking in a university amphitheater, which is, let us admit it, an unreal
setting. You thus dispose of the only criteria that permits recognizing if, in your exposé, you have said
something real or if you were satisfied merely by
words."*

As is so often the case, I will even say that
almost always, reflection cannot exercise itself
there where imagination is lacking, and I would
add, furthermore, that there is no charity, or *agapé*,
worthy of the name, without imagination.

* * * * *

In that experience of thinking, undertaken as I
have just described, it seems desirable to me to
start from a menace.

There cannot be Evil, if I am not mistaken,
unless a being is susceptible to being menaced. On
the other hand a menace is all the more menacing
insofar as it is more diffuse, as it is less able to be
circumscribed; and in that respect menace seems to

imply a certain confusion between what is within and what is without.

The person menaced is thus comparable to the defenders of a town under siege; the guardian of the town is not sure that the invader doesn't have accomplices within the town itself. He feels betrayed, but the uneasiness he feels in the face of this suspected, but not proven, betrayal adds even more to his trouble.

The word *trouble* here is very important. It seems that it's on this word that we must focus, if one intends to proceed with a questioning of Evil. On the contrary, if one abstracts from it, one places oneself outside the concrete situation of a human being struggling with Evil.

* * * * *

I would readily say that it's an encounter in the night, which would thereby distinguish it from all the encounters which can be made in the day; with someone that we see facing us and who can be recognized.

I shall invoke here the episode from *Sous le Soleil de Satan (Under the Sun of Satan)* by Georges Bernanos, in which the priest, Father Donissan, encounters the devil. Precisely because this encounter occurs during the night, it doesn't happen without the human being vacillating, and losing, or being on the point of losing, his equilibrium.

What is characteristic of Evil is to catch us off guard, or to *catch us in betrayal*, and that in a manner much too radical for us to possibly carry out the habitual task of localizing the guilty one.

This amounts to saying that it is entirely vain to imagine any possibility whatsoever of treating Evil like a character in a detective story, wherein Inspector X, by virtue of tenacity and astuteness, succeeds in identifying the author of the crime. To speak of the author of a crime is to introduce a certain duality between the agent and the act.

Every inquest postulates that duality is inevitably oriented toward the solution of the question: *who is it that . . . ?* And once that question is resolved, the detective can, and must, consider his job done. He doesn't need to reflect on the intimate relation, perhaps metaphysical, between the agent and the act. It's not exactly the same, at least apparently, in what concerns the judge and the jury, since they have to ask themselves if there are extenuating circumstances, if there is complete responsibility, etc.

Let us get back to what I called the encounter with Evil, through an example.

Here's a child who always had complete confidence in his parents. His mother had taught him that one should never lie. He never questioned the rightness of the commandment, even if he sometimes broke it; and if it happened that he himself lied, he knew that it was not good. But this conscience, more or less distinct, of doing Evil, has nothing in common with what I call the encounter with Evil.

Suppose now that one day he catches his mother in the flagrant delinquency of lying. Immediately he will literally no longer know where he stands or what to make of the situation. The being in whom he placed his confidence has betrayed him, or even worse, a source of values has been polluted.

Such a situation has, as its consequence, an impossibility to decide. Should he believe his mother is guilty because she has broken a rule whose value she herself has guaranteed; or should he think that on the contrary, the rule is in itself quite insignificant, and as a consequence the infraction or breaking it is also?

How then can he understand that this same rule as it was presented might not apply? Moreover, if the mother is guilty, how can he reconcile this discovery with his sentiments of respect and the admiration that people maintained for her? As the child, should I say to myself, that my mother is really someone like me; just as fallible as I am? And in that case, what attitude should I have toward her in the future? Is this the end of the respect that she had inspired in me? Has my mother, by that fact, ceased to be my mother?

* * * * *

I will now take up a quite different example, but one that can appear, to a certain degree, complementary to the previous one.

Several months ago, someone told me about a young man radiating strength and intelligence who seemed to promise a happy and fruitful life. Returning from vacation, experiencing I don't know what minor discomfort, he went to see his physician. He underwent certain tests and an X-ray, and these showed he had a form of cancer that develops ultra-rapidly and that his fatal end should come in less than a few months.

Here also, and perhaps more manifest than in

the previous case, it is clearly a question of an encounter with Evil. The Evil again this time presents itself as betrayal, or more exactly as being caught in betrayal. It's evident that it's not easy to give a name to what, in this instance, takes the place of the mother in the previous example; and besides an exact designation is not all that important. It's not even necessary to know if the young man was a believer or not, in the strict or confessional sense of the word. What we can say, with certainty, is that his life was directed by a sort of implicit confidence in powers that he didn't feel the need to name but whose harmonious cooperation assured the functioning of his faculties: and this cooperation was required in every case, whatever the faculties might be, just as much in the case of an athlete, an activist, a scientist, or an artist.

The sense of plenitude which accompanied his simplest endeavors was like an implicit assurance bearing upon this cooperation. He hadn't the slightest suspicion that this would be withdrawn from him. I shall repeat what I said earlier: It is obvious here that the distinction between what is external, and what is not, has practically no significance. One could say with indifference that everything is exterior, or that nothing is. But then it happens that in unforeseeable and scandalous circumstances this support is withdrawn.

A comparison comes irresistibly to mind, that of someone whose studies and living expenses, for example, were provided by a third party who suddenly without any discernible motive withdrew his financial support. The comparison will be all the more striking, if we suppose that the benefactor remained anonymous. Suddenly, there's nothing. The abandoned one writes, but no answer. The money was delivered through the intermediary of a notary who declares that he is not authorized to give the name of the donor. So, suddenly there's an incomprehensible emptiness. In the two cases, an indispensable assistance of which one believed himself assured, becomes missing; in both cases, there is no explanation, to the absolute disarray of the one abandoned.

Let us penetrate deeply the tragic, and in some respect unfathomable, sense of the word *disarray*. In both instances there is the same radical absence of recourse. In the case of the sick person, it's not only the fact that no one knows how to cure him; it's the lack of any response whatsoever to the maddening question: "why?" How can I understand how so many promises, which certainly appear to have been made, I don't know why or by whom, may be suddenly reduced to nothingness? Not only do I fail to succeed in fathoming what sense this frightful situation can have, but I cannot see if it has any sense whatsoever.

* * * * *

It's by starting from this situation, which people will recognize that I certainly have not tried to attenuate the poignant and extremely agonizing character, that we are led to ask ourselves, how Evil should be overcome.

Anyone who attempts to reflect philosophically on Evil, while dispensing himself from using an act of imagination, which regardless of what one may think of it, is inseparable from authentic charity – and in abstracting from this essential giveness which an encounter with Evil entails – one dooms oneself to remain outside the subject and fall short of the reality one wishes to investigate: because of this everything that he or she may say will be beside the point or more exactly without bearing on something which ceases to be a reality and so becomes merely a vague concept.

It seems to me that what one incorrectly calls "the problem of Evil" can only be encountered at the center of a concrete communication between one being and another.

It appears we are moving toward that philosophically unusual idea that we cannot effectively approach a being affected by Evil except on the condition that we enter into a relation with that person which, in the final analysis, is participation or communion. This means that this Evil should not, at all, remain for us an anomaly that should be explained away or reduced to relatively nothing.

* * * * *

The moment has come, I believe, to introduce a remark made in my presence by someone who, without being at all a professional philosopher, always seemed to me exceptionally insightful: *"Basically, there where Evil intervenes, Death inevitably begins its work. Evil announces Death; it already is Death."*

But here, once again, we must beware of distorting reductions which technical thinking tends toward, almost inevitably, for example, one that would consist in affirming that Death is part of a certain economy or even of an order that requires it. But just so, we see here, quite exactly here, how a falsifying substitution takes place – "the deceptive turn" – of which I've spoken many times. In such cases it's no longer a question of a particular Death *hic et nunc* (here and now) coming to devastate this concrete life, ruin this love, brutally interrupt this communion, but of Death in general, which concerns no person in particular and consequently about which one can comfortably discuss at all levels from the precisions of biochemistry up to the common themes of a certain moral philosophy. And that is not all; there is also a place here for a systematic sweetening. I have in mind that which expresses itself in a comforting spiritualism which believes it can domesticate Death, take away its sting, or even transform it into a simple game of hide and seek or of blind man's bluff.

Still I would not want people to misunderstand my thought on this point. For me there are powerful reasons for admitting that certain communions, apparently broken, can reestablish themselves beyond, as Mallarmé wrote "ce peu profound ruisseau calomnié, la mort" (that slandered shallow stream, Death). I also believe that there are graces and unforeseeable illuminations and that there would be everything to lose in pretending to find there nothing that resembles the technical successes susceptible to being obtained by no matter who, provided that he or she works at it with sufficient tenacity. There is here an extraordinary balance to preserve between childish gullibility, on the one hand and on the other, a systematic distrust which can degenerate into a veritable power of shutting out.

* * * * *

I spoke of illuminations: these liberating lights are there to assure us, or to confirm us in the assurance that there, where a proud and blind philosophy pretends to convince us that there is emptiness and nothingness – there is quite the contrary – a plenitude of life, the marvelous reserves of a world where promises abound, where everything that exists is called to a universal communion, where no possibility, no opportunity can be hopelessly lost.

Yet, our human structure is such that we can only know this immense creative consensus by a presentiment and, alas, infinite are the resources which despair has at its disposal to blind us to the ways these regenerative illuminations can come to us. So one must firmly declare that a philosophy which falls into the complacency of optimism, refusing to recognize the place of a temptation to despair, dangerously misunderstands a basic trait of

our human situation. In a certain way this temptation dwells, at the very center of our condition, yet
it still remains to discern if it is not a question of
the condition of humanity fallen and sinful.

Triumph of Evil – triumph of Death – triumph of despair: In truth these are the various
modalities of a unique and dreadful possibility
written on the horizon of *homo viator*, of one finding his or her path along a precarious narrow way,
the *chemin de crête* (road to Crete) between two
gaping chasms.

* * * * *

If I am engaged in struggling with Evil, such as I
have never ceased to describe it, that is, finally as
the temptation to despair of myself or of humans
or of God himself, it's not by folding back upon
myself that I shall succeed in overcoming this
temptation, for asphyxiation cannot be a liberation.

My only recourse is to open myself to a vaster,
and perhaps infinite, communion, at the heart of
which this Evil, which affected me, changes its
nature in some manner: for in becoming *our* Evil,
it ceases to be an attack focused on a love centered
on myself.

But that's not saying enough: It becomes the

Evil over which *thou, thou have triumphed*. Who is this *thou*? It's perhaps this person or that, whose example shines on the horizon of my memory, and we find here this recourse to the communion of saints, of which one will never recognize too explicitly the saving value. But it may also be – and besides in the final analysis, these are doubtless but two ways of expressing the same truth – beyond the level of this person or that person, The One who remains for us the Witness – the one whom every witness invokes, explicitly or not.

* * * * *

But, one might protest, is that not consecrating the failure of philosophy, in suspending it, in the last analysis, to Christian data?

Certainly, the objection deserves consideration in all its gravity, but the words *Christian data* could well present an ambiguity that it is important to disclose. Is it a question only of a certain miraculous story, whose authenticity, for those who do not consider it with the eyes of faith, does not appear irrecusable?

I think one must say this: what appears most evident to anyone who has meditated on the human condition, on human existence, is the fact that doubtless nowhere else, as much as in the Christian catechism, has the mystery of human existence been better clarified in its very depths. It follows from this that there exists no phenomenology of human existence that can exempt itself from evoking the double mystery of the crucifixion and the resurrection, uniquely able to project a light on our life, a light that gives it a sense.

The word *mystery* which I have just used is certainly the key word; and it's definitely here that we have to substitute the words *mystery of Evil* for the words *problem of Evil*.

In the face of the mystery of Evil, after so many alternative possibilities have evaporated, the only path remaining is that of a double affirmation, which must be preserved in its tension:

* Evil is real; we cannot deny this reality without undermining the fundamental seriousness of existence which cannot be contested without life's degenerating into nonsense or a kind of horrible buffoonery.
* And nevertheless, Evil is not real, *absolutely speaking*; we have to come not to a certitude, but to a faith in the possibility of overcoming it, certainly not just abstractly, in adhering to

a theory or to a theodicy, but *hic et nunc* (concretely here and now).

And this faith that is proposed to us is not without grace, it *is* grace; and what would we be, what would be the harassing journey that is ours, which is even our fashion of existing, without that Light which it is so easy to see and not to see, and which enlightens every human coming into this world?

* * * * *

(Written after the Massacre at Oradour.)[1]

They tell me that, alas the kind of metaphysical scandal that took place at Oradour produced the effects of Death that one could expect from it. More than one parishioner, from those days, turned away from the church, judging that on that awful day there burst forth, before everyone's eyes, either the non-existence or the absolute powerlessness of the God toward whom their prayers rose.

1 Oradour – A town remembered for the heinous barbaric massacre of 642 people (of whom 245 were women; and 207 were children) who perished in their own town church, which was deliberately burned. This heinous crime was done in retribution for resistance attacks against the occupying army.

It's no use shrugging one's shoulders. *That revolt, that refusal* are only too understandable. The theologian – I intentionally say the theologian and not only the Christian – is rigorously obligated to understand such an attitude, and *It's not a question here* of simply an intellectual comprehension, but rather of an act exactly like that of a dramatist who puts himself in the place of one of his characters regardless of who he or she may be. But I don't envision here a simple movement of compassion without doctrinal significance. The theologian is held responsible to ask himself or herself in all truthfulness if the notion of God, this theologian proposes, can withstand what I will call the ordeal of Oradour.

Let us not hesitate to say that if the traditional and confused category of objective causality is applied to God, this ordeal can really only lead to a disconcerting of one's faith. The pretense of God as prime mover and great engineer of the universe becomes almost fatally a God-object . . . a God-object who treats us as objects even in our inner depths, where any protestation attracts his punishment.

It's precisely starting with the idea of a God-object that a tragedy like that of Oradour becomes positively generative of atheism. Only, that idea of the God-object, even though theologians have for so long claimed the contrary, is actually incompatible with what is newest and most profound in the Christian message.

The Encounter Is an Appeal;
The Appeal Is an Encounter

A gift, no matter what it is, is never purely and simply received by a subject who would only have to make a place for it in himself.

The truth is much rather that the gift is an appeal, to which one is called to respond; it's as if it raised in us a harvest of possibilities, among which we will have to choose those that are most in accord with the solicitation addressed to us from within, and which basically is only a mediation between ourselves and ourselves.

* * * * *

Fortunately it can happen to each one of us to have an encounter, which comes breaking the routine ways of our egocentric landscape. From someone unknown, met haphazardly, there suddenly arises an irresistible appeal, to the point of overturning all the usual perspectives of our life's worldview, just as a gust of wind would overturn the panels of a stage's set.

What seemed close becomes infinitely distant and *vice versa*.

These are breaches, moreover, which close up again, most often, almost immediately.

Everyone can have had the experience of an encounter which reveals itself to have on his or her life indefinite, yet profound repercussions.

It's obvious that such a meeting presents each time, if you will, a problem; but we also see very clearly that the solution to this problem is situated beneath the question which alone is important. Suppose someone says to me, for example, *"You have met such and such, a person at a particular place because she loves the same kind of country or sea sites as you, or because her heath requires her to follow the same health treatment as you,"* one sees immediately that the response is non-existent.

In Florence or Engadine, there are crowds of people who are presumed to share my tastes. There are, at the spa where I go for treatments, a considerable number of sick people who suffer from the same problems as I do. But the presumed similarity of taste or illness does not draw us together in the real sense of the word; it has no connection with the intimate affinity, unique in its kind, which is at question here.

From this, it follows that I find myself in the presence of a mystery. Can we do away with the objection, declaring that there is nothing there after all but a lucky chance, a coincidence? A protest arises immediately from the depth of myself against that empty formula; against this ineffective negation of something that I apprehend at the very center of myself: I who ask myself what is the sense and the possibility of this encounter, I depend upon it, I am in some manner interior to it, it envelopes and comprehends me, even if I do not comprehend it.

Thus it's by a sort of denial or betrayal that I can say: *"After all, that could have not been. I would have remained all the same the person I was, the person I still am."* Neither should one say: *"I have been changed by this as by an external cause."* No, the encounter has developed me from within; it has affected me as a principle from within me.

* * * * *

Another example . . . everyday on the sidewalk or in the subway I rub elbows with hundreds of people I don't know, and this brushing past them is in no way an encounter. All these strangers present themselves to us basically as simply bodies occupying a certain place in the living space where we have to maintain ourselves and make our way.

Still it suffices that something which, objectively speaking, is nothing at all, for that level to be surpassed; for example, the tone in which as simple a phrase as *"I beg your pardon"* is pronounced, or the smile that accompanies it, and immediately a certain clarity appears, which has nothing in common with that of intelligence, but which can in a flash light up the obscurity, that is to say, above all, the solitude in which we try to feel our way ahead.

Suppose now that we meet again several days later *"by chance"* at the home of a third person, the person whose smile charmed us. *"This delight in meeting again"* will present itself to us as significant. And if someone disdainfully asserts that it's only a simple coincidence, we would have the distinct feeling, although unjustifiable, that the one who speaks that way falls short of the reality which does not allow itself to be reduced to its basic level; valid only for things that the word *coincidence* can designate.

Now this does not mean to say that we claim the right to build a sort of mythological explanation for this encounter but only that it situates itself at a level which is that of interiority, that is to say of *creative development.*

Very often, perhaps almost always, the refusal of an appeal takes the form of inattention; it's an inability to lend an ear to an interior voice, to an appeal addressed to the most intimate part of ourselves!

This inattention, this distraction, is a sort of sleep from which each of us can awaken ourselves at any moment. For this, it can be enough that the distracted person finds himself or herself placed in the presence of a person radiant with authentic faith; that faith which is a light and which transfigures the one in whom it dwells.

* * * * *

An authentic Christian experience is that of a saint, moreover just as much that of St. Vincent de Paul as that of St. John of the Cross. We see that it's an experience, confined as little as possible, to the limits of a subjectivity; quite the contrary, it's an experience that penetrates into its reality, orienting and transforming that reality.

What is important is to know what type of communication can be established between a

Christian experience understood in this way and, on the other hand, what can be a religious experience of another kind, rising from another doctrine (with reservations about the word doctrine), as for example that of a Buddhist.

To avoid contradictions that cannot be resolved for as long as one remains in the domain of "isms," for as long as one poses the problems in completely abstract terms, one must actually consider *encounters*. That the encounters might be possible, that they would be desirable, that they would allow for some type of communion richer and at times deeper than those known in the past, I profoundly believe . . . I believe there is a spiritual polyphony – which moreover cannot be easily established, because each one has, all the same, imperialist ambitions.

I Hope in Thou for Us

Hope is an expectation, but an active expectation which involves patience: now patience is something difficult and active.

Hope is the opposite of laziness and accommodation. This is something Péguy said clearly when he said that the soul who hopes is the opposite of "a soul who settles" or gets used to something.

Certain people seem incapable of hoping: it's like they lacked the faculty or capacity for it. Is it their fault? That seems very doubtful to me. It's as if they had a certain sort of paralysis, and I must say that these people are totally pitiable.

If one reflects on certain characteristics of World War II in Europe and if one considers the tragic condition of prisoners, one is led to ask oneself if hope couldn't be looked at, always, as an active reaction against a state of captivity. Perhaps we are only capable of hoping to the extent in which we first recognize ourselves as captives.

To hope is to carry within oneself the intimate assurance that, despite what appearances may be, the intolerable situation that is currently mine cannot be definitive; there must exist a way of escape.

* * * * *

Distinctive to hope is perhaps not being able to directly use or enlist any technique. Hope is proper to beings who are disarmed; hope is the arm of the disarmed, or, more exactly, hope is the opposite of a weapon and it is mysteriously in this that its effectiveness resides.

In certain cases, isn't it clear that the effectiveness of hope is in its disarming character? In opposing a force, that is to say, in placing myself on the same terrain as force, I tend to maintain it and to re-enforce it. It is true to say that any combat implies a sort of fundamental connivance between the adversaries, a common will that the combat endure, a will that cannot but present itself as legitimate defense. From this it follows that, if it meets non-resistance, there it is denied, there it is disarmed . . .

Hope is a surge; it is a soaring leap! It is not only a protestation dictated by love; it is also a sort of appeal, a boundless recourse to an ally who is also love.

* * * * *

Nature, unenlightened by hope, can only appear to us as a place of an immense and inflexible accounting.

The soul exists only by hope; hope is even the very stuff of which our souls are made. To despair of someone, isn't this to deny that person as having a soul? To despair of oneself, isn't that to commit suicide by anticipation?

* * * * *

Let us take despair. Here it's a question of the act

by which one despairs of reality as a whole; it presents itself as the consequence, or the immediate translation, of a certain accounting.

For as much as I can appreciate the real, I find nothing there that resists a process of dissolution; nothing which permits me to open a line of credit to it, no guarantee. It's a statement of absolute insolvency.

* * * * *

"Unhope." I tend to make myself unavailable to the precise extent in which I treat my life, or my being, as a quantifiable something I have, susceptible to being dilapidated, worn out, exhausted, or even vanishing into thin air.

I am going to find myself in the state of chronic anxiety of a person who is suspended over nothingness, who possesses a small amount of money, in total for everything, that he must make last as long as possible, for when it is spent he will have nothing.

That anxiety is worry, as gnawing, as a paralyzing element which serves to stop any enthusiasms and all generous initiatives. What must be seen is that this anxiety and worry can resolve itself into a state of inner inertia at the center of which the world is lived as putrescence and stagnation.

* * * * *

Hope is genuine hope only when it is surrounded by a halo, an aura of menace by despair.

* * * * *

But hope is essentially prophetic, which is in no way the case with desire.

It is in so much as hope is prophetic that hope transcends anxiety; this does not, of course, exclude for one who hopes and who remains a carnal creature, the fact of occasionally remaining, at inferior levels of himself, tributary to fear and anguish; but the part of the soul which hopes is, as it were, illumined by a light.

The only true authentic hope is one that relies on something that does not depend on us; hope's wellspring is humility, not pride, which consists in finding its strength in oneself alone. The latter attitude separates the one who experiences it, in that way, from a certain communion among beings, and tends thus to play its role as a principle of destruction. Moreover this destruction can be directed against oneself, because pride is in no way incompatible with self-hatred and can lead to suicide.

* * * * *

To love a being is to expect something from him, something indefinable, unforeseeable; it is at the same time to give him in some way the means to reply to that expectation.

Yes, as paradoxical as that may seem, to expect is in some manner to give; but the reverse is no less true: no longer to expect is to strike with sterility the being from whom one no longer expects anything. It is to deprive the other, to withdraw from the other in advance – what exactly – if not a certain possibility to invent or to create.

Everything permits thinking that one cannot speak of hope but where there exists that interaction between the one who gives and the one who receives, that community which is the mark of all spiritual life.

* * * * *

Christiane – We are not alone, no one is alone. There is a communion of sinners; there is a communion of saints.

Lawrence – One does not unite one's weaknesses. If one tries to do so, one cannot but mutually destroy one another.

* * * * *

Hope presents itself as piercing through time; everything happens then as if time, instead of closing off ones consciousness, lets something pass through it.

The prophetic character of hope. Doubtless one cannot say that hope sees what will be; but hope affirms as if it saw. One might say that hope draws its authority from a concealed vision the existence of which one is able to affirm without enjoying the detailed picture.

* * * * *

Now we come to the great question, the most important question, and it is Death. The situation of humans is such that they can find themselves affectively besieged by despair. A person can feel enveloped by despair. And I would say – not only as a Christian, but also as a metaphysician – that for me hope is the hope of salvation, being saved, being rescued, and I would say more exactly the hope for the resurrection.

This means that for me hope is, by its very essence and not in a contingent manner, hope in a world beyond. Death is really the threshold. Or one might use another image, the springboard.

The gate that bars the path of hope, but also the springboard that gives hope its momentum . . .

* * * * *

We will not be able to preserve the mysterious principle which is at the heart of our human dignity except on the condition of succeeding to explicate the properly sacred quality distinctive to it.

And this sacred quality appears, all the more clearly, as we stay increasingly close to a human being considered in its weakness, to the human being disarmed, such as we find him in children, in old people, and among the poor.

* * * * *

Whatever may have been our faults or our omissions, we have to remember with gratitude all that our short or long existences has been given to us by a power which it does not seem necessary to name, as the pledge and the seed of a life worthy of that name, that is both creative and fraternal.

I hope in Thou for us. I hope in Thou who are

the living peace, for us who are still fighting with ourselves and with one another, so that it can be given to us one day to enter into Thou and to participate in Thy fullness.

My Death in Me

We open ourselves in Death to that by which we have lived on earth.

* * * * *

There is one thing that I discovered after the Death of my parents; it is that what we call survivor (*survivre*) "one who lives after," is in truth, *sous-vivre*, "one who lives under"; and those whom we have not ceased to love with what is best in ourselves have now become as it were an invisible palpitating canopy, the presence of which is sensed, even lightly touched, under which we advance, even more bowed, always more detached from ourselves, toward the moment when everything will be swallowed up in love.

* * * * *

It is possible for me at every moment to detach myself enough from my life and see it as a succession of lots drawn. A certain number of drawings have already taken place; some other numbers must still appear. But what I have to recognize is that from the very moment when I was allowed to participate in this lottery a ticket was delivered to me on which my Death sentence appeared. The place, the date, and the manner of execution are not yet filled in.

It is obvious, on the other hand, that when I consider the lots that have befallen me in the past, I see that I cannot treat them as events that can simply be juxtaposed. The good and the bad chances react upon one another. I cannot even assign to these lots any fixed values. These could vary in function of lots that I have yet to draw.

I observe, furthermore, that the manner in which it was given to me to receive these successive drawings can appear to me too, as if by chance. Besides, here we enter into the indistinct, for it can seem that I must *be* before I can *receive*, but also that I can hardly hope to trace an exact line of demarcation between what I would confusedly call my nature, and the gifts or trials that have been dealt to me . . .

But in the midst of so many clouds that gather, one unchanging assurance remains: I shall die. That suffices for Death to impose itself on me as a fixed star among the universal scintillation of possibilities, and the fact that this is so can confer on my Death, in its relation to me, a sort of obsessive power and in some way petrifying. It may even happen that, overcome by dizziness, I yield to the temptation to put an end to this waiting, to this miserable respite the length of which I don't know, since I am in a situation entirely comparable to that of someone condemned to Death who can from one day to the next, from one minute to the next, see himself being taken to the place of execution.

"The moment when all is swallowed up in love" is not, if I may say simply "another event" purely descriptive of one in a sequence of events. It is beyond that. It is that in relation to which our existence can take shape and without which that same existence risks sinking into the absurd, and in the strong sense of the term into a decomposed cadaver.

This could lead to the recognition of what appears fundamental to me, that is, in its most profound perspective, the consideration of the Death of a loved one is infinitely more important than that of one's own Death.

I have insisted so much on that preeminence

for it to appear necessary to go back over it today. I shall simply recall the brief but extremely important controversy between Léon Brunschvicg and myself at the 1937 Congress of Philosophy. When he asserted that the Death of Gabriel Marcel seemed to preoccupy Gabriel Marcel much more than the Death of Léon Brunschvicg preoccupied Léon Brunschvicg; I answered him that he framed the question very poorly and that the only thing worthy of preoccupying either one or the other of us was the Death of the being whom we loved.

* * * * *

To love someone, is to say to that person: *"Thou, thou shall not die."*

* * * * *

I believe I can say that those who are no longer of this world, but who populate my heart, present themselves to me, ever more distinctly, if not as intercessors, at least as mediators, such that the reunions toward which I aspire, with all my being, can only find their meaning in the light of Christ.

The light of Christ: I experience a strange emotion in saying these words, for they mean for me something unusual, they signify that, for my spirit, the Christ is definitely less an object on which I could concentrate my attention than a Light which can, moreover, become a face, or more exactly a regard.

* * * * *

"You would not be satisfied with a world that mystery had deserted." The incomprehensible can send forth a light from the moment when it becomes the place of an authentic communion. If I remain Christian, it is, I believe, in spite of everything, because I adhere to the mystery of the communion of the suffering and its rootedness in the life and the person of Christ.

* * * * *

Spirit of metamorphosis,

when we try to push back the veil of clouds
which separates us from the other realm,
guide our novice gesture!

And when the appointed hour chimes, awaken in us
the light-hearted spirit of the traveler, who fastens on
his sack,
while outside the misted windows there appears
the gentle dawning of daybreak!

Bibliography

Works by Gabriel Marcel in English

Awakenings: A translation of Gabriel Marcel's auto-biography, En Chemin, vers quel eveil?), translated by Peter S. Rogers; introduction by Patrick Bourgeois; Marquette Studies in Philosophy 30 (Milwuakee: Marquette University Press, 2002).

Creative Fidelity, trans. by Robert Rosthal, introduction by Merold Westphal (New York: Fordham University Press, 2002).

Gabriel Marcel's Perspective on The Broken World; trans. by K.R. Hanley; Marquette Studies in Philosophy 18 (Milwaukee: Marquette University Press, 1998).

Gabriel Marcel Three Plays: A Man of God, Ariadne, The Votive Candle; introduction by Richard Hayes; A Mermaid DramaBook (New York: Harper & Row, 1965).

Ghostly Mysteries, The Mystery of Love and *The Posthumous Joke*; translated by K.R. Hanley; Marquette Studies in Philosophy 39 (Milwaukee: Marquette University Press, 2004).

Homo Viator: Introduction to a Metaphysic of Hope, 2nd edition, translated by Emma Craufurd and Paul Seaton (South Bend, Ind.: St. Augustine's Press, 2009).

Man against Mass Society, trans. G.S. Fraser; foreword by Donald MacKinnon (South Bend, Ind.: St. Augustine's Press, 2008).

The Mystery of Being, in 2 vols.: Vol. I: *Reflection and Mystery,* trans. by G.S. Fraser; Vol. II: *Faith and Reality,* translated by G.S. Fraser (South Bend, Ind.: St. Augustine's Press, 2001).

A Path to Peace: Fresh Hope for the World. Dramatic Explorations by Gabriel Marcel's dramatic explorations throughout five plays: *The Heart of Others, Dot the I, The Double Expertise, The Lantern,* and *Colombyre or the Torch of Peace,* translated by K.R. Hanley (Milwaukee: Marquette University Press, 2007).

Presence and Immortality, trans. by Michael A. Machado, revised by Henry J. Koren (includes: "My Fundamental Purpose," 1937; "Metaphysical Journal" (1938–1943), "Presence and Immortality" 1951, originally entitled Existential Premises of Immortality; and *The Unfathomable*, an unfinished play, March, 1919) (Pittsburgh: Duquesne University Press, 1967).

Selected Works about Gabriel Marcel

Thomas Anderson, *A Commentary on Gabriel Marcel's* The Mystery of Being, 2 vols.; Marquette Studies in Philosophy 46 (Milwaukee: Marquette University Press, 2006).

Lewis E. Hahn and Paul Arthur Schilpp, eds., *Gabriel Marcel*; The Library of Living Philosophers 17 (LaSalle, Ill.: Open Court Publishing Company, 1984).

Biographic Note

Gabriel Marcel was born in Paris, December 7, 1889, and died in Paris on October 8, 1973.

His father Henry Marcel, Member of the Cabinet and a Diplomat, became the Administer of the National Library, Director of the National Museums, and Minister of Fine Arts. His mother, Laura Meyer, born into a family of Israelite Bankers, died in 1893, and Gabriel Marcel was raised by his aunt Marguerite Meyer.

After having received an Aggregation in Philosophy, Gabriel Marcel taught at Vendôme, in 1912, then at the Condorcet Lyceum, from 1915 to 1918. During the war, he directed a service of the Red Cross assigned to find combatants missing in action.

In 1919, he accepted a teaching position at Sens and married Jacqueline Boegner, daughter of Alfred Boegner and cousin of Marc Boegner. She died in 1947.

In 1921 he began to work with the *Nouvelle Revue Française* and there met Charles du Bos. The following year, he became part of a committee of readers for Plon and for Grasset Publishers. He wrote the theatre column for *L'Europe Nouvelle* and wrote articles and reviews for *Sept, Temps Présent,* and *La Vie Intellectuelle.*

In 1925, a first play by Gabriel Marcel, *La Chapelle Ardente (The Votive Candle* or *The Funeral Pyre),* was staged by Gaston Baty at the Théâtre du Vieux Colombier. Several years later, in 1938, *Le Fanal (The Lantern)* was performed at the French National Theater, La Comédie Française.

In 1929, in response to an invitation by François Mauriac, he converted to Catholicism and received baptism March 23rd. In 1934 he met Gaston Fessard, S.J. and began to participate in meetings of the Oxford Groups and to receive German writers and philosophers including Joseph Roth, exiled by the Nazis. Starting in 1936 there began the series of "Fridays," informal meetings of philosophers and students who gathered at his home, 21 rue de Tournon. Gabriel Marcel, in 1940–1941, got to know Jean Grenier and Edmond Michelet then, in 1946, met Heidegger in Fribourg.

For all that Gabriel Marcel did not renounce his passion for the theatre. Between 1949 and 1953 three major plays – *Un homme de Dieu, Rome n'est plus dans Rome, le Chemin de Crête (A Man of God, Rome Is No longer in Rome, Ariadne)* are performed in major theaters. During this same time 1945–1965 he was the regular drama critic for *Nouvelles Littéraires.*

Many awards and prizes were conferred upon him: in 1949 the French Academy's Grand Prize for Literature; in 1952 election to the Academy of Political and Moral Sciences; in 1958 the National Prize for Literature; and in 1969 the Erasmus Prize.

Index